The Best Sacred Piano Solos
Selected by Lloyd Larson

Table of Contents

AMAZING GRACE (Arr. Johnson) 14
COME, YE THANKFUL PEOPLE, COME (Arr. Larson) 2
DEEP RIVER (Arr. Christopher) 18
JESUS IS ALL THE WORLD TO ME (Arr. Bolks) 10
GOD OF OUR FATHERS (Arr. Larson) 34
PRAISE TO THE LORD, THE ALMIGHTY (Arr. Bock) 38
SING WE NOW OF CHRISTMAS (Arr. Larson) 8
THOU ART WORTHY (Arr. Lucas) 21
WERE YOU THERE? (Arr. Larson) 26
WONDERFUL WORDS OF LIFE (Arr. Curry) 30

Fred Bock Music Company
www.FredBock.com

COME, YE THANKFUL PEOPLE, COME

with "Now Thank We All Our God"

GEORGE J. ELVEY
and JOHANN CRÜGER
Arranged by LLOYD LARSON

Gently, slower (♩ = ca. 96)
mf
p
cresc.
mp
mf
f

32
35
Regally (♩ = ca. 92)
ff
rit.
38
41
44
mf

48
51
f
54
ff
57
molto rit.
fff

SING WE NOW OF CHRISTMAS

Traditional French Carol
Arranged by LLOYD LARSON

17
8va
p
pp
21
mf
dim. e rit.
Slowly, freely (♩ = ca. 88)
mp
25
29
holding back
moving ahead
cresc. e accel. poco a poco
33
mf

37
f
41
ff
44
rit.
12
ten.
Tempo primo (♩ = ca. 112)
mf
47
f
mf
f
51
mf
mp

54
mf
58
f
62
ff
66
rit.
70
black note gliss.
molto rit.

JESUS IS ALL THE WORLD TO ME

WILL L. THOMPSON
Arranged by DICK BOLKS

17
rall.
21
mp a tempo
25
29
mf
rall.
33
mp a tempo
rall.

37
mf a tempo
41
45
49
rall.
53
mp
a tempo
mf

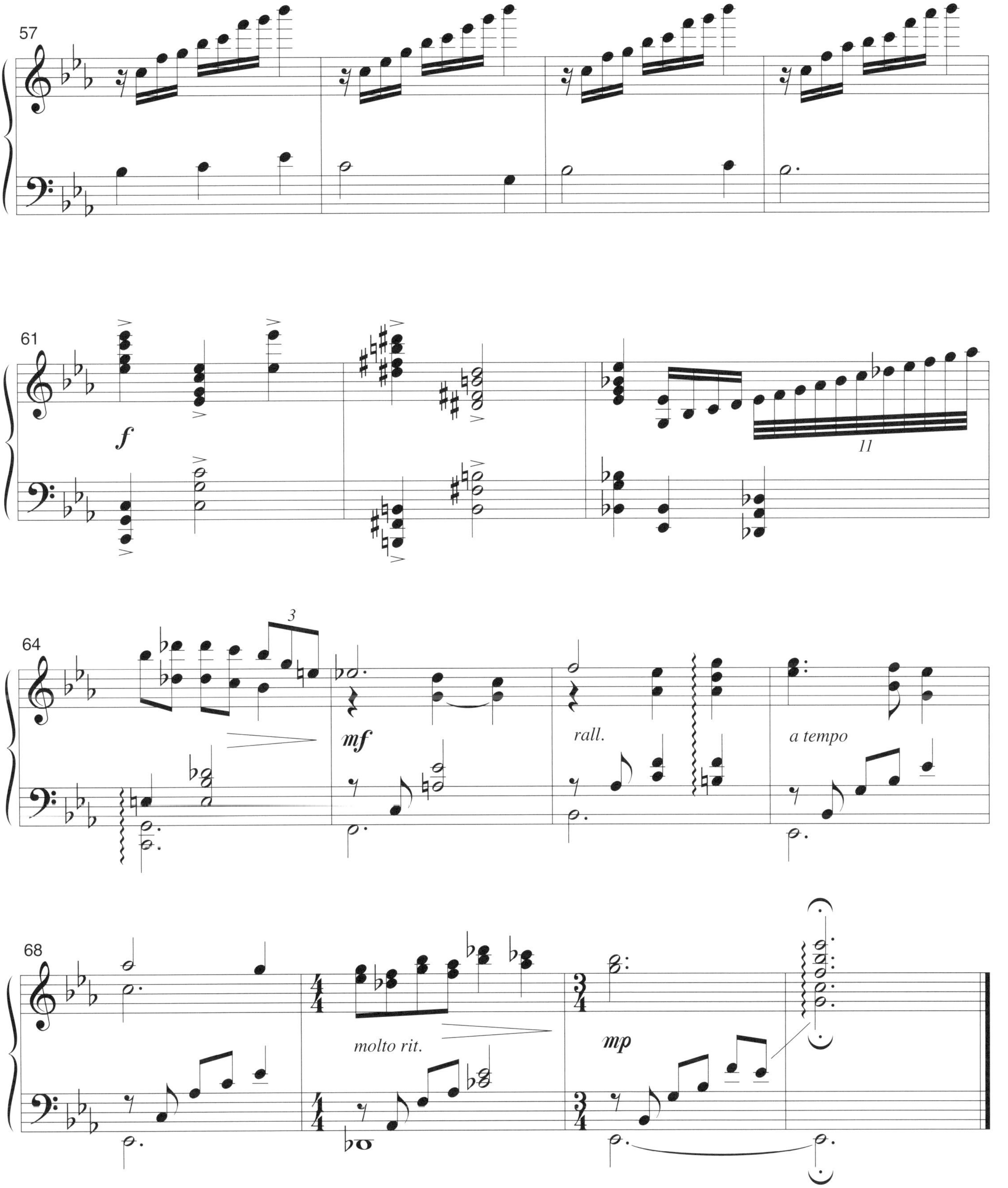
57
61
f
11
64
3
mf
rall.
a tempo
68
molto rit.
mp

AMAZING GRACE

Traditional American Melody
Arranged by PAUL JOHNSON

12
Flowing
16
rit.
mf
19
A little faster
22
25
A little slower

28
31
34
f
rall.
37
accel.
40

43
3
3
rall.
mf
3
3
46
3
3
49
3
mp
52
mf
55
mp rit.
p
8va

DEEP RIVER

with "Shall We Gather at the River?"

African American Spiritual
and ROBERT LOWRY
Arranged by KEITH CHRISTOPHER

Very free and expressive, unrushed (♩ = ca. 60)

13
16
19
22
mf moving ahead
cresc. poco a poco
25
f
holding back

28
dim. poco a poco
mp
31
mf a tempo
cresc. poco a poco
34
8vb
f
37
mf
p

THOU ART WORTHY

PAULINE MICHAEL MILLS
Arranged by JIM LUCAS

Majestic, bold and accented (♩ = 76)

17
21
25
f
29
p
mp
mf
33
f

37
p
p
mf
mf
41
mf
45
49
rit.
Broader
f
53

57
mf
61
65
p
mp
mf
69
f
73
p
p
mf
mf

77
mf
81
Like the beginning (bold, accented)
f
85
rall.
89
molto rit.
ff
fff

WERE YOU THERE?

African-American Spiritual
Arranged by LLOYD LARSON

16
p
20
6
mp
rit.
23
more motion
26
mf
29
cresc.
f

32
mf
35
dim.
p
39
43
mf
46
3
3
3
f

49
ff
6
52
dim.
55
mf
ff
3
58
mf
62
dim. e rit.
p very freely
molto rit.

WONDERFUL WORDS OF LIFE

PHILIP P. BLISS
Arranged by CRAIG CURRY

Gently, reflectively, with rubato (♩ = 60)

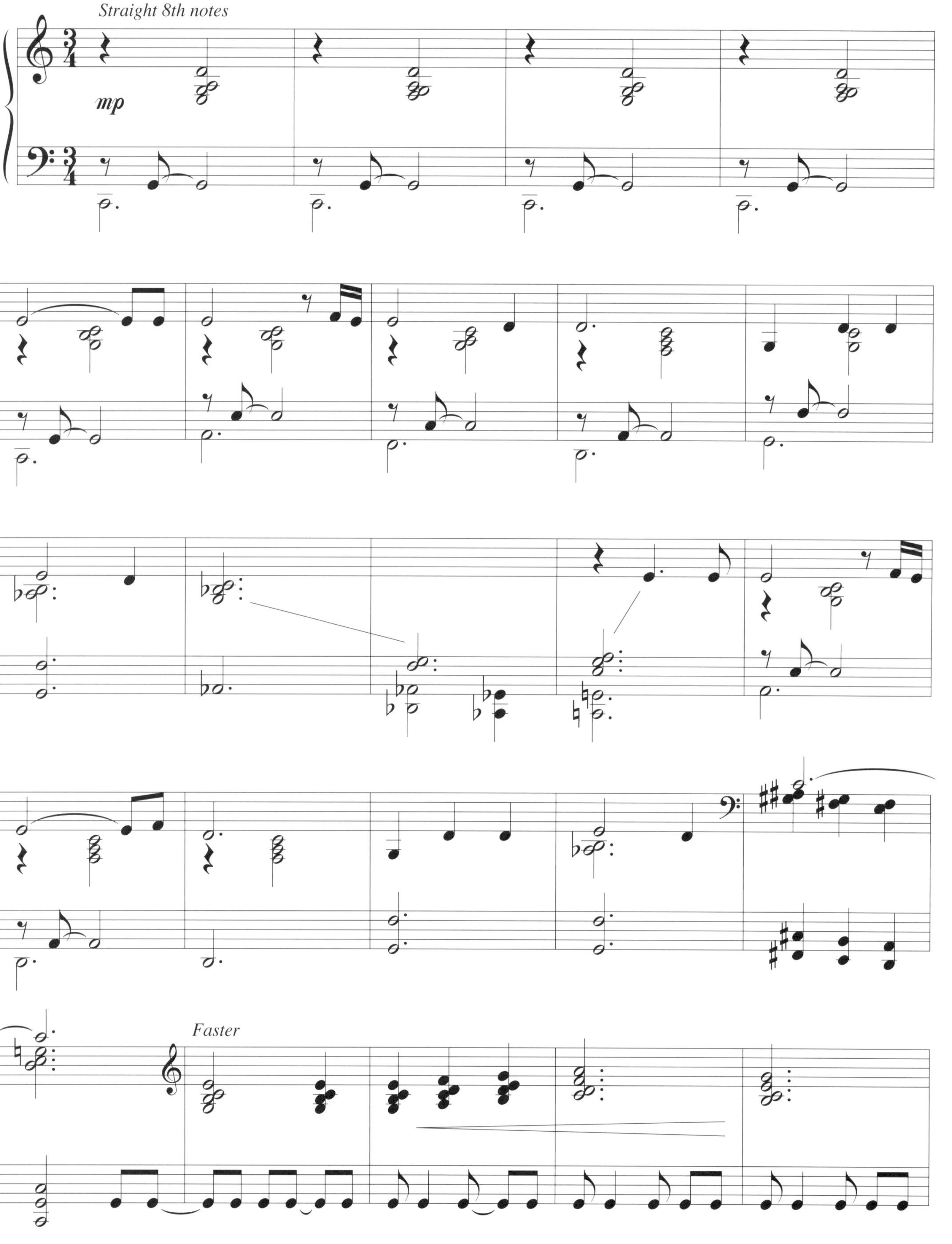

25
f
mf
rit.
mp a tempo
30
35
rit.
a tempo
40
44
rit.

48
53
mp
58
63
Faster
mf
68
f

72
mp
77
mf
rit.
mp
a tempo
82
87
mp
92
p
rit.
R.H.
pp
8va

GOD OF OUR FATHERS

GEORGE W. WARREN
Arranged by LLOYD LARSON

17
20
3
23
26
mp
30

34
mf
38
f
41
44
47
cresc.
rit.
Broadly (♩ = ca. 96)
ff

51
55
58
61
65
rit. poco a poco al fine
cresc.
fff

PRAISE TO THE LORD, THE ALMIGHTY

Stralsund Gesangbuch
Arranged by FRED BOCK

24
30
35
mf
mp
39
mf
f
p
45
legato
mf
mp

51
p
mp
mf
f
rit.
ff
56
Full and Strong
f
62
Stately
mf
67
mf
lightly
mp
72
mf
77
f
ff